ZIDIK.IZ

iPhone 15 Senior Guide

Discover the Excitement: Explore the Amazing Features of iPhone 15 – Your Guide to Innovation, Style, and Ultimate Performance.

First edition

This book was professionally typeset on Reedsy.
Find out more at reedsy.com

Contents

1

Introduction

W elcome to the world of the iPhone 15 Senior Guide – a friendly companion designed to help you navigate the exciting features of your new iPhone with ease. In this chapter, we'll take a stroll through the landscape of smartphones, specifically focusing on the iPhone 15. No tech jargon, just a simple and engaging conversation about what makes this device special and why this guide is here for you.

Overview of the iPhone 15

Let's start by looking at the iPhone 15 itself. If you've been part of the iPhone family for a while, you'll appreciate the journey it has taken. From the early models that revolutionized how we communicate to the sleek and sophisticated iPhone 15, each iteration has brought something new to the table.

The iPhone 15 isn't just about keeping up with the times; it's about understanding its users. Apple has crafted this device with thoughtful features that cater to a senior audience. We're talking about larger text, clearer icons, and functions designed to make your experience smoother and more enjoyable.

Evolution of iPhones

Think back to the first time you held an iPhone – it was a game-changer, wasn't it? The journey from basic calls and texts to a device that practically fits the world in your pocket has been remarkable. The iPhone 15 continues this legacy, building on years of innovation to bring you a smartphone that doesn't just keep up; it understands your needs.

Notable Features

Now, let's talk about what sets the iPhone 15 apart. It's not just a sleek design and a high-quality camera (although those are certainly impressive). The standout feature here is the intentional design with seniors in mind. Apple has listened to your preferences, offering larger text and clearer icons to make navigation more straightforward. The iPhone 15 is not just a phone; it's a companion tailored to enhance your digital experience.

Target Audience

Now that we've got a sense of the iPhone 15, let's talk about who this guide is for – you, the senior user. We're not defining seniors by a number; we're celebrating the wealth of experience and wisdom that comes with a bit more life lived. This guide is for those who may be new to the world of smartphones or are looking to sharpen their digital skills.

Defining the Senior Audience

Being a senior doesn't mean fitting into a stereotype. It means having a unique perspective shaped by experiences. This guide recognizes that perspective and aims to cater to your specific needs and preferences. It's not about limitations; it's about embracing the unique qualities that come with age.

Tailoring the Guide

Consider this guide your friendly tech companion – we're here to make the journey enjoyable. We've avoided complex tech jargon, opting for clear and straightforward language. It's like having a conversation with a friend who understands your perspective and wants to help you navigate the digital landscape at your own pace.

Importance of a Senior-Friendly Guide

Now, you might wonder, why a guide specifically for seniors? Let's delve into that.

Digital Inclusion for Seniors

The digital world is expanding rapidly, and smartphones are at the forefront of this evolution. We believe in exclusivity, ensuring that everyone, regardless of age, has the opportunity to participate in this digital revolution. Using a smartphone isn't just a trend; it's a gateway to connecting with loved ones, accessing information, and being an active part of the global conversation.

Building Confidence

We get it – technology can be a bit overwhelming. But fear not, because this guide is here to boost your confidence. We want you to feel comfortable using your iPhone 15 for various tasks – from sending messages to making calls and capturing special moments with the camera. It's not just about learning; it's about empowering you to enjoy the benefits of technology.

Guide Navigation Overview

Now, as you embark on this journey with your iPhone 15 Senior Guide, let's talk about how you'll navigate through the chapters.

Outlining the Structure

Consider this guide your roadmap through the world of iPhone 15. We've organized the content into chapters and sections, making it easy for you to find the information you're looking for. Whether you're setting up your iPhone 15 or exploring its camera features, we've got everything neatly arranged to guide you on your journey.

Tips for Optimal Learning

Learning something new takes time, and that's perfectly fine. We encourage you to go at your own pace, take breaks, and practice what you've learned. Learning about your iPhone 15 should be an enjoyable experience, not a source of stress. Embrace the process, and you'll find yourself mastering your device in no time.

We're not here to throw information at you, we want this guide to be interactive and enjoyable.

Interactive Elements

Throughout the guide, you'll find little quizzes, tips, and hands-on exercises. It's like a mini adventure – you get to explore your iPhone 15 while having some fun along the way. And if you have questions or need clarification, don't hesitate to reach out – we're here to assist you.

Personal Stories

To make the journey even more relatable, we've sprinkled in some stories from fellow seniors who've embraced technology. These are real people, sharing their genuine experiences. It's a way to show that you're not alone in this journey, and there's a supportive community cheering you on. Your exploration of the iPhone 15 is part of a broader narrative of seniors embracing technology, and we're thrilled to have you as a part of it.

In essence, welcome to the iPhone 15 Senior Guide – your companion for a delightful exploration of the exciting world of smartphones. It's a journey filled with discovery, empowerment, and a touch of tech magic. Let's embark on this adventure together.

2

Getting Started

Congratulations on your new iPhone 15! In this chapter, we'll guide you through the initial steps of unboxing and setting up your device. Whether you're a first-time iPhone user or upgrading from an earlier model, we've got you covered. Let's dive into the exciting world of your iPhone 15.

Unboxing, Charging, and Setting Up the iPhone 15

The unboxing experience is like opening a treasure chest, and at the heart of it is your new iPhone 15. Before you start exploring its features, it's essential to ensure your device is charged. Locate the charging cable and power adapter in the box. Connect the lightning cable to the charging port at the bottom of your iPhone 15 and the other end to the power adapter. Plug it into a power outlet, and let the device charge for a while.

The charging process is relatively quick, allowing you to get started in no time. While it charges, take a moment to appreciate the sleek design and the vibrant display that awaits you.

Turning it On and Off

Once your iPhone 15 has sufficient charge, it's time to power it on. Locate the power button on the right side of the device. Hold it down until the Apple logo appears on the screen. Your iPhone is coming to life!

To turn off your iPhone, press and hold the power button again until you see the "slide to power off" slider. Swipe it, and your device will gracefully shut down. Knowing how to power your device on and off is the first step in mastering its basic functions.

Creating an Apple ID

To unlock the full potential of your iPhone 15, you'll need an Apple ID. This ID acts as your passport to the Apple ecosystem, allowing you to download apps, make purchases, and sync your data across devices. If you already have an Apple ID, you can sign in. If not, you can create one during the setup process.

Follow the on-screen instructions to connect to Wi-Fi, set up Touch ID or Face ID for added security, and choose whether to restore from a previous device or set up as a new iPhone. The setup process is intuitive, guiding you through each step with clear instructions.

Navigating the Home Screen

With your iPhone 15 all setup, let's take a closer look at the home screen – your gateway to the world of apps and functionalities.

Understanding Icons and App Layout

The home screen is where you'll find all your apps neatly arranged in a grid. Each icon represents a different app, and you can customize the layout based on your preferences. Tapping an icon opens the corresponding app. If you find an app you want to use frequently, you can move it to the dock at the bottom of the screen for easy access.

Customizing the Home Screen

Rationalization is key, and your iPhone 15 allows you to make it your own. Press and hold on any app icon until it starts wiggling. This indicates that you're in editing mode. From here, you can rearrange apps by dragging them around, create folders for better organization, or even delete apps you no longer need.

Accessing Control Center and Notifications

Swipe down from the top-right corner of the screen to access the Control Center. Here, you'll find quick settings like WI-Fi, Bluetooth, and screen brightness. It's a convenient way to toggle essential features without diving into the settings menu.

Notifications, on the other hand, are accessed by swiping down from the top of the screen. This area shows your recent notifications, keeping you updated on messages, emails, and other app alerts. Understanding how to navigate these features ensures you have quick access to essential settings and stay informed about your device's activity.

Now that you've unboxed, set up, and explored the basics of your iPhone 15, you're ready to dive into specific functionalities and make the most out of your device. In the upcoming chapters, we'll delve into essential apps for seniors, accessibility features, and much more. Remember, it's a journey of discovery, and we're here to guide you every step of the way.

3

Essential Apps for Seniors

Welcome to Chapter 3 of the iPhone 15 Senior Guide! Now that you've got your device set up, it's time to explore the essential apps that will make your iPhone experience even more enjoyable. In this chapter, we'll focus on the fundamental applications that seniors often find valuable – from making calls to capturing memories with the camera. Let's dive in!

Phone and Contacts

Making and Receiving Calls.

The Phone app is at the core of your iPhone's communication abilities. Making a call is as simple as tapping the green phone icon, selecting a contact, and hitting the call button. If you receive a call, swipe the green answer icon to pick up, or the red icon to decline.

For added convenience, your iPhone 15 allows you to make Face Time calls – a video calling feature that lets you connect with friends and family face-to-face, even if they're miles away. Simply tap the Face Time app, select a contact, and choose either a video or audio call.

Managing Contacts

Keeping your contacts organized is essential. The Contacts app on your iPhone allows you to store names, phone numbers, and email addresses. To add a new contact, open the Contacts app, tap the "+" icon, and fill in the details. You can also import contacts from other devices or apps.

For those with a long list of contacts, the search feature comes in handy. Just tap the search bar at the top of the Contacts app, enter a name, and quickly find the person you're looking for.

Using Face Time

Face Time is more than just a video calling app; it's a way to stay connected with loved ones. Open the Face Time app, choose a contact, and start a call. Face Time is great for virtual gatherings, allowing you to see and talk to multiple people at once. It's like having a family reunion right on your iPhone!

Messages and Email

Sending and Receiving Messages.

Texting has become a universal way of staying in touch, and the Messages app on your iPhone 15 is your gateway to this digital communication. To send a message, open the app, tap the compose icon, select a contact, and start typing. You can add emojis, and photos, and even use the voice-to-text feature for hands-free messaging.

Incoming messages will appear as notifications on your screen. Simply tap the notification to open the Messages app and respond. Group messages are a fun way to chat with multiple people at once, perfect for coordinating plans or sharing updates.

Composing and Managing Emails

If you prefer email for more formal communication, the Mail app has you covered. Open the app, tap the compose icon, and enter the recipient's email address. Type your message, add any attachments, and hit send. You can organize your emails into folders for better management and mark important messages for quick access.

The Mail app supports multiple email accounts, so whether you use Gmail, Yahoo, or another provider, you can centralize your email experience on your iPhone.

Understanding Emoji and Stickers

Emojis and stickers add a fun and expressive touch to your messages. In the Messages app, tap the emoji icon to access a vast array of emojis that go beyond the traditional smiley faces. You can also download sticker packs from the App Store to enhance your messaging experience. It's a lighthearted way to convey emotions and make your messages more engaging.

Camera and Photos

Taking Photos and Videos.

The Camera app on your iPhone 15 turns your device into a powerful tool for capturing moments. To take a photo, open the app, frame your shot, and tap the shutter button. For videos, switch to video mode and press the red record button. The iPhone 15's advanced camera features ensure your photos and videos are crisp and vibrant.

Organizing and Editing Photos

The Photos app is your gallery, where all your captured memories reside. You can organize your photos into albums, making it easy to locate specific moments. If you want to edit a photo, simply open it in the Photos app, tap "Edit," and use the intuitive tools to adjust brightness, crop, or add filters.

Using iCloud for Photo Storage

With iCloud, you can securely store your photos and videos in the cloud, freeing up space on your device. To enable iCloud Photo Library, go to Settings, tap your name, select "iCloud," then "Photos," and toggle on iCloud Photos. This ensures that your precious memories are backed up and accessible across all your Apple devices.

This concludes Chapter 3 of the iPhone 15 Senior Guide. We've covered the essential apps that will empower you to communicate, connect, and capture moments with your device. In the next chapters, we'll explore accessibility features, internet and social media usage, and much more. Remember, your iPhone is not just a gadget; it's a gateway to a world of possibilities, and we're here to guide you every step of the way.

4

Accessibility Features

Welcome to Chapter 4 of the iPhone 15 Senior Guide! In this chapter, we'll delve into the accessibility features that make your iPhone experience inclusive and tailored to your unique needs. Apple is committed to ensuring that everyone, regardless of abilities, can use their devices comfortably and effectively. Let's explore the accessibility features that will enhance your iPhone 15 experience.

Enlarged Text and Display

One of the standout features for seniors is the ability to enlarge text and adjust the display settings for better visibility. To enlarge text, go to Settings, tap "Display & Brightness," and choose "Text Size." Here, you can adjust the slider to increase the text size throughout your device, making it easier to read messages, emails, and other content.

For an even more tailored experience, explore the "Display & Text Size" settings. Here, you can choose larger text options and bold text to enhance readability. The iPhone 15 empowers you to customize the display to suit your preferences and ensure a comfortable viewing experience.

VoiceOver and Speak Screen

For those who prefer auditory assistance, VoiceOver and Speak Screen are powerful tools. VoiceOver is a screen reader that narrates what's happening on your device, making it accessible to users with visual impairments. To enable VoiceOver, go to Settings, tap "Accessibility," then "VoiceOver," and toggle it on.

Speak Screen, on the other hand, reads the content of your screen aloud. To activate Speak Screen, go to Settings, tap "Accessibility," then "Spoken Content," and toggle on "Speak Screen." Now, you can swipe down with two fingers from the top of the screen to have your iPhone read the content to you. These features open up a world of possibilities for accessing information without relying solely on visual cues.

Magnifier and Zoom

The iPhone 15 includes features designed to assist with magnification, particularly beneficial for reading small text or examining details. The Magnifier function turns your device into a magnifying glass. To enable Magnifier, go to Settings, tap "Accessibility," then "Magnifier," and toggle it on. Now, you can triple-press the side or home button to access the Magnifier and use your camera to zoom in on objects.

Zoom, another helpful tool, allows you to magnify the entire screen. To activate Zoom, go to Settings, tap "Accessibility," then "Zoom," and toggle it on. You can adjust the level of zoom by double-tapping the screen with three fingers and then moving them up or down. These features provide a flexible and customization way to enhance visibility.

Hearing and Interacting with Siri

The iPhone 15 ensures that users with hearing impairments can fully engage with their devices. Live Listen, an accessibility feature, turns your AirPods or compatible hearing aids into a remote microphone. To use Live Listen, go to Settings, tap "Accessibility," then "Hearing," and enable Live Listen. This feature is particularly useful in noisy environments or when you want to focus on specific sounds.

Siri, your virtual assistant, is another valuable tool for hands-free interaction. To activate Siri, simply say, "Hey Siri" if your device supports the feature, or press and hold the side or home button. Siri can perform a wide range of tasks, from sending messages to setting reminders, making it convenient for users with mobility or dexterity challenges.

In this chapter, we've explored the accessibility features that empower seniors to make the most of their iPhone 15. Whether it's enlarging text, using VoiceOver, or interacting with Siri, these tools are designed to enhance usability and cater to diverse needs. As we continue our journey through the iPhone 15 Senior Guide, we'll explore internet and social media usage, health and wellness features, and much more. Your iPhone is not just a device; it's a gateway to a more accessible and inclusive digital experience, and we're here to guide you every step of the way.

5

Internet and Social Media

Welcome to Chapter 5 of the iPhone 15 Senior Guide! In this chapter, we'll embark on a journey through the realms of the internet and social media using your iPhone 15. Whether you're exploring websites, connecting with friends on social platforms, or discovering new interests, your device is your gateway to the digital world. Let's dive in and make the most of your online experience.

Safari Browser Basics

The Safari browser on your iPhone 15 is your window to the internet. Navigating through websites is a breeze, and we'll guide you through the basics.

Navigating Websites

Open Safari by tapping its icon on the home screen. You'll see the address bar at the top, where you can enter a web address or search keywords. Once on a website, you can scroll up and down by swiping with your finger. To zoom in on a specific area, pinch the screen with two fingers, and to zoom out, reverse the pinch gesture.

Managing Bookmarks

Bookmarks are like digital shortcuts to your favorite websites. To bookmark a page, tap the share icon at the bottom of the screen (it looks like a square with an arrow pointing up), then select "Add Bookmark." You can access your bookmarks by tapping the book icon at the bottom, making it easy to revisit your preferred sites.

Searching the Web

The search bar in Safari is your key to exploring the vast expanse of the internet. Tap the bar, enter a search term, and Safari will generate relevant results. You can also use voice search by tapping the microphone icon on the keyboard and speaking your query.

Using Social Media Apps

Social media brings people together, and your iPhone 15 allows you to stay connected with friends and family on various platforms. Let's explore the basics of using social media apps.

Facebook, Twitter, and Instagram Basics.

Facebook is a versatile platform for sharing updates and photos and staying in touch with loved ones. To use Facebook on your iPhone, download the app from the App Store, login or create an account, and start exploring your feed.

Twitter, known for its concise updates, is another popular social platform. Download the Twitter app, sign in or create an account, and start following accounts of interest. You can share your thoughts through tweets and engage with others by liking and retweeting.

Instagram, a visual-eccentric platform, is perfect for sharing photos and videos. Get the Instagram app, login, or create an account, and start sharing your moments. You can follow friends, family, and accounts that align with your interests.

Posting and Interacting with Content

Posting on social media is a great way to share your experiences. To post on Facebook, tap the status update box, write your message, and add photos or videos if desired. For Twitter, tap the tweet icon, compose your tweet, and add media if needed. Instagram lets you share photos and videos by tapping the "+" icon, selecting your media, and adding a caption.

Interacting with content is equally important. On Facebook, you can like, comment, and share posts. Twitter allows you to like, retweet, and reply to tweets. Instagram offers likes and comments on photos and videos. The social media landscape is about connecting and engaging with others, and your iPhone makes it effortless.

Privacy Settings

Understanding and managing privacy settings is crucial when using social media. On Facebook, you can customize your privacy settings by tapping the three horizontal lines, selecting "Settings & Privacy," and navigating to "Privacy Shortcuts." Twitter and Instagram also offer privacy settings within their respective apps. Take the time to explore these settings and tailor them to your comfort level.

6

Managing Health and Wellness

Welcome to Chapter 6 of the iPhone 15 Senior Guide! In this chapter, we'll explore the health and wellness features that your iPhone 15 offers. From tracking physical activity to monitoring health metrics, your device can be a valuable companion on your journey to well-being. Let's dive into the world of health and wellness with your iPhone 15.

Health App Overview

The Health app on your iPhone is a comprehensive hub for tracking various aspects of your well-being. Let's start by exploring its core features.

Tracking Physical Activity.

Physical activity is a key component of a healthy lifestyle, and the Health app helps you monitor your movement. Open the Health app, navigate to the "Browse" tab, and select "Activity." Here, you can view details such as step count, distance traveled, and flights climbed. The app also tracks your daily activity levels, providing insights into your overall fitness.

To make the most of this feature, ensure that you've set up the Health app with accurate information about yourself, including age, gender, and activity level. The app uses this data to provide personalized insights tailored to your specific needs.

Monitoring Health Metrics

The Health app goes beyond basic activity tracking, allowing you to monitor various health metrics. Navigate to the "Health Data" tab and explore categories such as "Vitals," "Results," and "Reproductive Health." Here, you can input data manually or connect compatible devices to automatically track metrics like heart rate, blood pressure, and more.

The Health app acts as a central repository for your health information, offering a holistic view of your well-being. You can set goals, receive insights, and track your progress over time. It's a powerful tool for proactively managing your health.

Emergency SOS Feature

Your iPhone 15 includes the Emergency SOS feature, designed to provide quick assistance in critical situations. To enable Emergency SOS, go to Settings, tap "Emergency SOS," and toggle on "Call with Side Button" if it's not already activated.

In an emergency, press the side or home button five times rapidly to initiate an emergency call. Your iPhone will automatically dial the local emergency services number and share your location with them. This feature adds an extra layer of security, ensuring that help is just a few taps away.

Medication and Appointment Reminders.

Managing medications and keeping track of appointments can be challenging, but your iPhone 15 simplifies this process with helpful reminders.

Setting Medication Reminders.

To set up medication reminders, open the Health app, navigate to the "Health Data" tab, and select "Medication." Here, you can add your medications, including dosage and frequency. Once added, the Health app can send reminders to take your medications on time, ensuring that you stay on top of your prescribed regimen.

Using the Calendar for Appointments

Your iPhone's Calendar app is a handy tool for managing appointments and scheduling health-related activities. Whether it's a doctor's appointment, a fitness class, or a wellness checkup, you can add events to your calendar and set reminders. Open the Calendar app, tap the "+" icon to create a new event, and enter the details. You can customize reminders to receive alerts before your scheduled appointments.

7

Troubleshooting and Support

Welcome to Chapter 7 of the iPhone 15 Senior Guide! In this chapter, we'll explore troubleshooting techniques and the support options available to you. While your iPhone 15 is designed to be user-friendly, occasional issues may arise. Fear not, as we're here to guide you through common problems and connect you with the support you need.

Common Issues and Solutions.

Let's address some common issues that users may encounter and discuss solutions to troubleshoot them.

Battery Drain

If you notice that your iPhone's battery is draining faster than usual, there are a few steps you can take to improve battery life:

Check for apps running in the background and close unnecessary ones. Adjust screen brightness and use the Low Power Mode feature. Update to the latest iOS version, as updates often include optimizations for battery performance.

Slow Performance

If your iPhone is running slower than expected, consider the following: Clear cache and unnecessary files by deleting unused apps. Restart your iPhone to refresh system resources. Ensure you have the latest software updates installed.

Connectivity Issues

Issues with Wi-Fi or cellular connectivity can be frustrating, but there are ways to troubleshoot:

Toggle Airplane Mode on and off to reset connections. Forget and reconnect to Wi-Fi networks. Restart your iPhone and check for carrier settings updates.

App Crashes

If an app is crashing or behaving unexpectedly, try the following. Close the app and reopen it. Check for app updates in the App Store. Delete and reinstall the problematic app.

Storage Full

Running out of storage space can impact your iPhone's performance. To free up space:

Delete unused apps and media files. Use the "Optimist iPhone Storage" feature in Settings > Photos. Transfer photos and videos to iCloud or a computer.

Unresponsive Screen

If your iPhone screen is unresponsive, consider these steps:

Restart your iPhone by holding down the side or home button. If using Face ID, ensure your face is visible to the camera. Update to the latest iOS version.

Contacting Apple Support

If you encounter persistent issues or need personalized assistance, Apple provides various support options:

Apple Support App

The Apple Support app is a convenient way to get help on your terms. Download the app from the App Store, sign in with your Apple ID, and access a range of support resources. You can chat with Apple Support, schedule a call, or browse helpful articles tailored to your device.

Online Resources and Community Forums.

Apple's website offers a wealth of information, including support articles and community forums. If you prefer self-help, you can explore troubleshooting guides and discussions on the Apple Support Community. Fellow users and Apple experts often share insights and solutions to common issues.

Genius Bar Appointments

For in-person assistance, you can schedule an appointment at an Apple Store's Genius Bar. The Apple Store app allows you to book a time slot, and a knowledgeable Apple technician will assist you with any hardware or software concerns. Remember to back up your data before any appointment involving device inspection or repair.

Phone Support

If you prefer speaking with a support representative, Apple provides phone support. You can find the appropriate contact number for your region on the Apple Support website. Be ready with your device's serial number and a description of the issue to streamline the support process.

8

Staying Safe and Secure

Welcome to Chapter 8 of the iPhone 15 Senior Guide! In this chapter, we'll focus on essential tips and features to ensure the safety and security of your device and personal information. Your iPhone 15 comes equipped with robust security measures, and understanding how to use them effectively is crucial for a worry-free digital experience.

Passcode and Face ID & Touch ID

Your first line of defense is securing your iPhone with a passcode, Face ID, or Touch ID. Let's explore these security features.

Passcode

A passcode is a numeric or alphanumeric password that grants access to your iPhone. To set or change your passcode, go to Settings, tap "Face ID & Passcode" or "Touch ID & Passcode," and follow the prompts. Choose a secure passcode that's easy for you to remember but difficult for others to guess.

Face ID

Face ID is a facial recognition feature that uses your face to unlock your iPhone. To set up Face ID, go to Settings, tap "Face ID & Passcode," and follow the on-screen instructions. Ensure that your face is well-lit during the setup process for accurate recognition.

Touch ID

If your iPhone has a Touch ID sensor, you can use your fingerprint to unlock it. To set up Touch ID, go to Settings, tap "Touch ID & Passcode," and follow the instructions to enroll your fingerprints. This method provides a quick and secure way to access your device.

Two-Factor Authentication

Two-Factor Authentication (2FA) adds an extra layer of security by requiring a secondary verification step in addition to your password. Enable 2FA for your Apple ID to protect your account and connected devices.

To enable 2FA, go to Settings, tap your name at the top, select "Password & Security," and then "Turn on Two-Factor Authentication." Follow the prompts to set it up. With 2FA, even if someone has your password, they would still need a secondary verification code to access your account.

Find My

The Find My app is a powerful tool for locating your iPhone in case it's lost or stolen. Let's explore its features.

Locate Your iPhone

To use Find My, ensure it's enabled in Settings > [your name] > Find My. If your iPhone is lost, open the Find My app on another Apple device or use the Find My website on a computer. Sign in with your Apple ID, and you'll be able to see your device's location on a map.

Play a Sound or Mark as Lost

If your iPhone is nearby, you can play a sound to help locate it. If your device is lost, you can activate Lost Mode, which locks your iPhone and displays a custom message with contact information. This feature is particularly useful for increasing the chances of someone returning your lost device.

Erase Your iPhone Remotely

In extreme cases where recovery is unlikely, you can remotely erase all the data on your iPhone using the Find My app. This ensures that your personal information remains secure. Note that this action is irreversible, so use it with caution.

App Permissions and Privacy Settings.

Managing app permissions and privacy settings is crucial for controlling the information apps can access on your iPhone.

Review App Permissions.

Regularly review the permissions granted to each app on your device. Go to Settings, scroll down, and select each app to review and modify its permissions. Disable access to features that aren't necessary for the app's core functionality.

Location Services

Be mindful of location services and grant access only to apps that genuinely require your location. In Settings, go to Privacy > Location Services to manage which apps can access your location and when.

Avoiding Scams and Phishing

Staying vigilant against scams and phishing attempts is essential for maintaining a secure digital environment.

Recognizing Scams

Be cautious of unsolicited messages or calls claiming to be from reputable organizations. Legitimate entities won't ask for sensitive information via email or phone calls. If in doubt, contact the organization directly using verified contact information.

Email Safety

Avoid clicking on links or downloading attachments from unknown or suspicious emails. Be wary of phishing attempts that mimic official communications. Verify the sender's email address and reach out to the organization independently if needed.

Software Updates

Regularly updating your iPhone's software is a fundamental step in maintaining security. Apple releases updates to address vulnerabilities and enhance overall device performance.

To check for updates, go to Settings > General > Software Update. If an update is available, follow the prompts to install it. Enabling automatic updates ensures that your device stays protected with the latest security patches.

Emergency SOS and Medical ID.

Your iPhone includes features designed to assist in emergencies.

Emergency SOS is activated by pressing the side or home button five times rapidly. This initiates a call to local emergency services and shares your location. Make sure Emergency SOS is set up in Settings > Emergency SOS.

Medical ID.

Medical ID provides critical information about your health that can be accessed even when your iPhone is locked. To set up Medical ID, open the Health app, tap your profile picture in the top-right corner, and select Medical ID. Here, you can enter details such as medical conditions, allergies, and emergency contacts.

9

Recap and Ongoing Learning

Congratulations on reaching the final chapter of the iPhone 15 Senior Guide! Throughout this guide, we've embarked on a journey to help you master your iPhone 15, exploring its features, apps, and functionalities. In this concluding chapter, let's recap the key points covered and encourage ongoing learning and exploration.

Recap of Key Points

Unboxing and Setting Up: We began our journey with the excitement of unboxing your iPhone 15. From charging the device to creating an Apple ID, you learned the essential steps to set up your device.

Navigating the Home Screen: Understanding the home screen layout, icons, and customization options allows you to personalize your iPhone for easy access to your favorite apps.

Essential Apps for Seniors: We explored fundamental apps like Phone, Messages, Email, Camera, and more. You discovered how to make calls, send messages, and capture memories with the camera.

Accessibility Features: Chapter 4 focused on accessibility features, empowering you to tailor your iPhone experience to your unique needs. From enlarged text to VoiceOver, these features enhance usability.

Internet and Social Media: Chapter 5 delved into the world of the Internet and social media. You learned to navigate Safari, use Facebook, Twitter, and Instagram, and connect with friends and family.

Health and Wellness: In Chapter 6, we explored the Health app, which helps you track physical activity, monitor health metrics, and set reminders for medications and appointments.

Troubleshooting and Support: Chapter 7 equipped you with troubleshooting techniques for common issues. We also discussed the various support options provided by Apple, from the Apple Support app to Genius Bar appointments.

Staying Safe and Secure: Chapter 8 focused on security measures, including passcodes, Face ID, Touch ID, Two-Factor Authentication, and features like Find My. We also discussed privacy settings, avoiding scams, and the importance of software updates.

Now, let's emphasize the importance of ongoing learning and exploration.

Ongoing Learning

Technology is ever-evolving, and there's always something new to discover. Here are a few tips for ongoing learning with your iPhone 15:

Stay Updated.

Keep your iPhone's software up to date by regularly checking for updates in Settings > General > Software Update. Apple releases updates with new features, improvements, and security patches. Enabling automatic updates ensures you're always on the latest version.

Explore New Apps

The App Store is a treasure trove of apps catering to various interests and needs. Explore new apps to enhance your iPhone experience. Whether it's for learning, entertainment, or productivity, there's an app for almost everything.

Join Online Communities

Connect with other iPhone users in online communities or forums. Platforms like the Apple Support Community provide a space to ask questions, share experiences, and learn from fellow users. You might discover tips and tricks you didn't know existed.

Attend Workshops or Classes

Local Apple Stores often offer workshops or classes on using Apple devices. Check their schedule for events tailored to seniors or beginners. These sessions provide hands-on learning and an opportunity to ask questions directly.

Experiment and Customize

Your iPhone is a versatile device with many features waiting to be explored. Don't hesitate to experiment with settings, try out new gestures, or customize your device to suit your preferences. The more you explore, the more confident you'll become in using your iPhone effectively.

10

Conclusion

As we wrap up the iPhone 15 Senior Guide, remember that your iPhone is not just a device; it's a gateway to a world of possibilities. From staying connected with loved ones to managing your health and exploring the vast expanse of the internet, your device empowers you to lead a fulfilling digital life.

We hope this guide has been a valuable companion on your journey of discovery and mastery. If you ever encounter new challenges or have questions in the future, don't hesitate to explore the support options provided by Apple or reach out to the online community.

Your iPhone 15 is a tool for connection, learning, and enjoyment. Embrace the ongoing adventure of exploring its features and capabilities. Happy exploring, and may your iPhone journey continue to be a source of joy and empowerment.

If you found this book useful. I'd be very appreciative if you left a favorable review for the book on Amazon. Thank you so much.